YOU
MATTER
It Doesn't

YOU MATTER

It Doesn't

LEAVING YOUR

"*It*"

BEHIND

Bobby Petrocelli

HONOR✠NET
PUBLISHERS

SAPULPA, OKLAHOMA

You Matter, It Doesn't

ISBN 978-1-938021-37-4
Copyright © 2015 by Bobby Petrocelli
www.10seconds.org

Published by HonorNet Publishers
P.O. Box 910
Sapulpa, OK 74067

Dedication

Debra (Debbie) Ann Petrocelli
March 2 1957–December 28, 2014

To my beautiful sister
So loved, so missed!

The beauty of Debbie Petrocelli will always shine
in our lives…forever and always! We are all better
people for having experienced her love!

Debbie truly lived the following: "You will never go
wrong having a heart of generosity. Give first!"

How Debbie treated all of us screamed out, "You
matter!" or as we say in Brooklyn, "Youz matta!"

CONTENTS

... ⎯⎯⎯⎯ ...

Prologue

THIS MOMENT MATTERS

••• ———————————— •••

My whole life I have heard the expression, "Take life one day at a time." Throughout all of my experiences, my short comings, and my victories I realize that this statement is in fact, the furthest thing from the truth. Why is that? Life doesn't *happen* one day at a time—it is *lived* one moment at a time. Lives are changed in *one moment*, not in one day. *Carpe momento; cease the moment!* Lives are measured in *moments!* There is power in every moment, and a great importance in every single decision we make. I like to call it *"present moment awareness"*! The fact that you are reading this book, you are in the *right* place, at the *right* moment right *now!* Hopefully this will become an *unforgettable* moment for you.

Every moment has the power to not only impact your life but also to profoundly impact the lives of others. When we serve others we show our strength. Every decision we make—whether good, bad, right, or wrong—has the potential influence to greatly impact us all. Each choice can literally change our lives. Our *responses* to all that we have faced in life has brought us to this particular point. It's a timeline—a process. We are all in this *present* moment because of every decision that either we or others have made. Life is truly about moments of impact. Each moment is important.

How we see ourselves, how we see others, how we believe others see us, and how we believe God sees us influence our decisions. Our perception of the world around us has great sway. Time and again good people have bad moments. Often one word, one decision, and one moment can define and describe how we see all things.

One of my favorite words is *epiphany*. It can be described as "a sudden realization," "a light goes on," "an aha moment," or "a God wink," in which we tend to have a clearer vision of something in our lives. Several years ago I had the privilege of spending a week on the campus of the University of Miami in Coral Gables, Florida. I was honored to address each of the school's athletic teams. The last team to hear me speak was the women's basketball team. Prior to me addressing the women, the head coach shared a little of their recent court woes. The Lady Hurricanes had lost six straight games to start the new year. Not a very happy way to begin a new year. They had been a .500 team but had hit a slippery downhill slope from which they just couldn't pull themselves out. They were to play Top 10 nationally-ranked ACC opponent Georgia Tech that night. The odds makers were particularly harsh and declared Miami to be a 25-point underdog in the game. The coach mentioned how many of the young women were making poor on-court decisions. With a sense of urgency in her voice she said, "Bobby, please, I need your help in any way." This certainly seemed to be a pivotal point in their season. If they didn't turn it around soon, it would be very tough to reverse the losing momentum. I could feel the raw emotion in the room.

When I addressed the team the very first thing I asked them was if they knew what the word *epiphany* meant. They responded with "a sudden realization," "an *aha* moment where the light goes on," and "a defining decision and defining moment." I told them, "There are several awesome definitions for this very powerful word." I proceeded to tell them, "This moment right now—today—can be an epiphany for you. For each of you individually it's that time. But more importantly as a team—it's that time." As every eye was fixed on each word I spoke, I proclaimed to them, "You can turn around your season and the life of this team. You can do it, but you have to see it. Do you see it? I see it. I want you to have the epiphany that I see. I want it to be as clear to you as it is to me." And then it happened. It was almost as if the dark clouds of losing and negativity had suddenly split and the bright sunshine of optimism and winning had broken through. To this day, I can almost see the angels descending through the clouds singing like a choir. "Ahhhh—ahhhhh—ahhhhh—ahhhhh!" And you know what? They saw it too! They saw it! They not only saw it, but they also embraced it. Like a refreshing cool rush of wind, the negativity was completely blown out of the room and replaced with a positive, winning spirit. There was freshness in the air. It was that dramatic. The entire room was changed. When I finished speaking, the players approached me one by one to thank me for encouraging them. I could see the change in their demeanor and the hope in their eyes. They had found themselves again, both individually and as a team. Even their physical posture had changed. No more slumping shoulders. No more weight of the world on their backs. They had been renewed—invigorated. They had a complete change of attitude. It permeated the room.

Because of my busy speaking schedule that week, I couldn't stay in Coral Gables to watch the game. Later that night I drove to the Miami airport to catch a flight back home to the Tampa area.

At approximately at 9:05 p.m. I got a text message from my friend Steve Debardelaben at U of M. His text read, "Bobby, you are not going to believe it. One of our girls just hit a 3 pointer at the buzzer. We just beat Georgia Tech, 54-52." Wow! What?! Are you kidding me? Are you serious?! I was elated to say the least. I texted Steve back immediately and asked him to please tell the team how excited and proud I was for them. Approximately twenty minutes later his second text read, "Epiphany...the girls and the coaches want to truly thank you." What a great feeling to know that they not only understood, but they also lived the power of the epiphany. What a great feeling to know somehow I had an impact on them. It doesn't get better than that!

The next morning I woke early, still filled with excitement for the Miami women's victory, I literally ran to get the morning paper, the *St. Pete Times*, off my front porch. I turned immediately to the sports section and focused on the ACC basketball pages. I began to read the article about the Miami-Georgia Tech women's game. The article told how Miami was down by 10 points at halftime. The coach decided to play a freshman point guard throughout the second half. The article continued to say how this freshman scored the final 10 points for Miami, including the game winning 3-point basket at the buzzer. As I continued to read, I was shocked, blown away...frozen in my tracks. It was right in front of me in black and white print. I couldn't believe that the preceding day, nobody from the University of Miami could have told me this. Life is unbelievable. This freshman point guard had not played that much throughout the entire season, then the coach put her in for the second half and she played incredibly. That's amazing in itself, but that's not what amazed me the most. I couldn't believe what I was about to read. No one from the Miami basketball team told me this at any time, in any conversation, in any way whatsoever. This little used freshman player who hit the huge 3 point shot to win the game after leading her team back from a 10 point halftime deficit—and after Miami was a huge 25 point underdog to nationally ranked Georgia Tech—her name was *Epiphany*! "Steve, are you kidding me?" What?! Wow! Unreal!

Several weeks later Coach Frank Haith invited me to address the University of Miami men's basketball team (Jimmy Graham, a New Orleans Saints tight end was a member of the team) before they played sixth ranked Duke. My message that night was simple. I shared about *Epiphany* from the women's team. I can tell you the Miami men's team played so great and beat powerful Duke in overtime. You can't make it up. Life is sometimes unpredictable. As Dick Vitale would say, "Awesome, baby!"

When Derek Jeter retired from the Yankees, he played the last game of his career at rival Red Sox's Fenway Park. One of the most amazing tribute and farewell signs that encapsulated

Derek's baseball life along with life in general stated, "Don't cry that Derek is leaving baseball, but rejoice and be thankful you got to experience him for the last twenty years!" Life is truly a journey, not a destination! This is *your* moment, *your* magical moment! Start right now. This is *your* time! This can be your second chance by making a second choice. Don't wait for the changes to come. You can change the way you play the cards you are dealt. For decades scientists have believed that genes give rise to everything in your life. Your genetic thumbprint is what is going to happen. The field called genetics says, "This is your destiny!" Not true! There is a growing field called epigenetics. It says if I change my lifestyle and do things differently, I don't have to have the same future or outcome that my family has experienced. If my family has been affected by heart disease, I don't have to! I can change genetic codes by changing lifestyle choices. I can alter my destiny! Action will bring change. What are you waiting for? This book can be your epiphany! Don't miss this moment! An improved *you* is the objective!

Chapter 1

WHO DO YOU THINK YOU ARE?

··· ———————————— ···

How do you see yourself? Be honest. If you were to look in the mirror for a good, long look, how would you describe what you see? The way we see or view ourselves is extremely important. It's called our self-concept. Literally, it is the concept of yourself, the concept of you. Like looking at yourself from the outside as others see you. If you were to stand back and see yourself this way, how would you say that you look? Are you beautiful? Are you cute? Are you handsome? Are you intelligent? Are you funny? Or do you think of yourself as stupid, ugly, or boring? How would you describe yourself? What physical attributes and personality traits would you mention are the most prominent in describing you? How do you *see* things? How you perceive yourself and your place in the world is an important question to honestly ask. That's why my goal is TCL: *Think, Choose, Live*! If we change the way we think, we'll change the choices we make. And if we change the choices we make, we'll change the life we live!

Unfortunately, many of us do not have a good or positive self-concept of how we see ourselves. Why is this? Why don't we have a more positive view of ourselves and who we actually are? What lies have you bought into about who you are? Often we are not honest about who we are, but rather who we *think* we are. We see ourselves as who we would like to be. If you are reading this, you are still here, and I want you to hear! You haven't given up, and you haven't failed. You are not a failure. There's a very thin line between success and failure. No matter what anyone tries to tell you, there are no overnight successes. It only seems that way.

Upcoming music artists, groups, boy bands, rappers, actors, and star athletes sometimes seem to come out of nowhere to enjoy super-stardom. And although they do appear to become instant celebrities, they are not. Many years of hard work and hours upon hours of sacrifice went into their careers before they "suddenly" ascended to the top of their respective field. Overnight successes many times actually take ten or more years to reach that point. Celebrities often joke in TV interviews that it took them "ten or twenty years to become an overnight success." They worked extremely hard to attain what they have in their careers. If you ask a successful person how many times they failed before they finally found success, most will tell you that they struggled tremendously for a long time before great things started to happen. It's a process. It's a journey. It's a mountain to climb. Most successful people have been knocked down many times for many years, but the secret is that every time they were seemingly knocked out cold on the canvas, they were always willing to get back up and dust themselves off one more time. That's what it takes. No matter how many times they were down for the count, they always got back up. They had no "quit" in them. It wasn't in their mental DNA. They didn't allow failure to become part of their internal vocabulary. It wasn't in their life's dictionary. There's an old expression that says something like this, "We choose how we see ourselves, just like others choose how they want to see us." More often than not we tend to see ourselves the way we think others see us. When our self-concept is no longer how we view ourselves, we have allowed others to determine how we view who we are. We permit others to determine our destiny by what they say or how they have treated us. Why are we allowing others to determine this? Why are we giving them that power? Eleanor Roosevelt famously said, "No one can make you feel inferior without your consent."[1] We always return to the protected mode of how we see ourselves.

Baseball has always been my all-time favorite sport. I played all through high school in New York City and even into college for one of the top NCAA Division I baseball teams in the country. During my college career, my teammate and buddy Mike Moore was drafted overall #1 in the Major League Draft by the Seattle Mariners. Mike would later win a World Series Championship with the Oakland A's as one of their star pitchers.

I've experienced some truly amazing things in my life, but I have to say it is an absolute miracle that I am alive today after growing up in Brooklyn, New York. God's country! Brooklyn in the house! LOL! If you ever go to Brooklyn, make sure you bring a camera. It's a special place. You will see things—I promise—that you will never, ever see again in your life, starting with your camera. But even though I am a native New Yorker, as a kid my favorite baseball team—and one of the reasons I just said that it's an absolute miracle that I am alive today, because, as a kid, I was a Boston Red Sox fan. Yes, that's right. I was a Sox fan. Think about that. In New York? Yes, I was! My father's younger brother, my uncle, was Rico Petrocelli, the Red Sox All-Star shortstop who played for them during my childhood years in the 60s and 70s. You can imagine me and my friends continually battling over who was better—the Sox or Yanks. Good thing for me that in the years that my uncle Rico played, Boston mostly won. And he was a big reason why they were so good.

Several years ago, Uncle Rico and his son, my cousin Michael, were working in Florida. Since I live there it was a great opportunity to catch up with them while they were in the area. Uncle Rico had been associated with the Ted Williams Hitters' Hall of Fame and Museum which is now located in Tropicana Field—home of the Tampa Bay Rays. My son Alec and I planned to meet them there. While touring the museum, I spotted one of my favorite historical Red Sox players of all time, Dominick DiMaggio. Wow! Dom was the brother of Joe DiMaggio, the Yankee great who famously had the 56-game hitting streak, the longest in the Major Leagues. So I grabbed my son's hand and walked him over to see Dom to possibly get an autograph. My heart was racing as I was filled with awe and excitement. I walked up to him and said, "Mr. DiMaggio, I'm Rico Petrocelli's nephew. May I please have an autograph for my son Alec?" His response was, "I don't give a blankity blank blank that you are Rico Petrocelli's nephew. My whole life all I ever heard was that I was Joe DiMaggio's brother. Who are you?" "I am Bobby Petrocelli, and this is my son Alec." His response back to me was very quick and matter-of-fact, "It is a pleasure to meet *you*, Bobby and Alec Petrocelli. Not because you are Rico Petrocelli's nephews, but because you are Bobby and Alec Petrocelli. I want to give you an autograph because of who *you* are, not who you are with"! It was an encounter I will never forget. He wanted to meet me and my son for who we were. Not because of our association to my uncle. Me for me! I'll never forget that. His actions screamed out, *you matter!*

So who do you think you are? What or who defines you? I am who I think I am. You have great importance. You have great worth. You have great value. You are a human *being*, not a human *doing*! You already have a valuable life's position that your performance can't change.

Your fingerprints define who you are physically. They separate you from everyone else. Not one of the billions of people on this earth has *your* exact fingerprint. It's unique and specific to you and only *you*! That's incredible when you think about it. I hope that you always will know that there is something absolutely incredible about you. No one shares your fingerprint. No one. Not one single person. That's pretty special. It's specialized to you. You are one in seven billion. Infinitely rare. You are that special. You are priceless, you are unique, and there is no one in the world like you. *You matter!* We in New York say, *"youz matta!"* You have a plan and a destiny that no one else can fulfill except you.

Each of us has a light inside us. You have a light burning in you. Be led by the guidance of that light, and the inner voice that is there as well. It can be heard softly and oftentimes comes in a whisper. Stillness allows us to hear the inner voice of the pilot light burning. Live from within. We already have a great vision within. Vision tailors our behavior. We head in the direction we look. Be defined by what is in you.

Everyone matters and wants to be loved. People want to feel loved and accepted, and they want to have a sense of importance. No one wants to be rejected.

Love never rejects. No one can really reject us since we have the highest form of acceptance. God doesn't reject us.

One of my favorite rock songs, from one of the greatest rock bands of all times, is the anthem of the whole world. The band Foreigner's song, "I Want to Know What Love Is" is the cry of *everyone*! They want to know love! More songs have been written about love. We wouldn't strive and ask for love if it were not everything to us. We base our value on how loved we perceive we are. Love is everything to everyone. Feeling loved and sensing we are loved is vital.

One of my favorite movies of recent history is the Best Picture Academy Award Nominated film *The Help*. The movie, with ensemble cast, is about a young white woman and her relationship with two black maids during the American civil rights era (the early 1960s). Abby, one of the two maids, is caring for a little white girl. Her relationship with her is so special, as she continually tells the little girl, "you is smart, you is kind, you is important."[2] It's a powerful line in the movie. She simply told this child, "You are loved" because *you matter*! Many voices are speaking to us in this world on a daily basis. What voice are you listening to and not just hearing? Do you know there is a difference between hearing and listening? There is! Hearing is simply the act of perceiving sound by the ear. If you are not hearing-impaired, hearing simply happens. Listening, however, is something you consciously choose to do. Listening requires concentration so that your brain processes meaning from words and sentences. Listening leads to learning. There are two types of listening skills: passive and active. Passive listening takes little effort and little attention. You are not really paying attention. An example would be having some ambient music playing in the background while you do something else, like read or surf the web. Or if you have the television on, but only for the background noise that it emits, not for actually watching what's on it. Active listening is making a concerted effort to pay attention to, think about and process, and actually retain what you hear. The voice we actually listen to and don't just hear, confirms how we distinguish ourselves.

Sylvester Stallone, in an interview on *The Tonight Show* told host Jimmy Fallon about the time he auditioned for the now famous role of Hans Solo in *Star Wars*. He talked about sitting down and reading for director George Lucas and how he could tell from the beginning that things were not going well and that the vibes he was getting in the audition were immediate, that he was not right for the part. Stallone went on to say that after the audition, which went poorly, he jokingly said to Lucas, "That's okay; I don't look good in spandex anyway.[3] The coveted role of Hans Solo went to a dashing, young actor named Harrison Ford and ultimately made him a huge action star. Stallone, of course, went on to win an Academy Award for his iconic film *Rocky* which he wrote and starred in. George Lucas clearly didn't see Sylvester Stallone as his heroic character Hans Solo. But can you imagine if Lucas had cast Stallone instead of Harrison Ford in *Star Wars*? It would have been an entirely different film all together. The setting might have been a rundown neighborhood in South Philly. His character might have been named Hands So Low. Instead of Chewbacca the Wookie, his sidekick might have been named Butkus the Dog. Princess Leia might have been Princess Adrian—and her iconic hair buns on each side that covered her ears would have been Cat Glasses and fifteen Intergalactic sweaters. Burt Young could have played Luke Side Walker. Alec Guiness's character Obi Wan Kenobi's name might have been Obi Want Pierogi. I can hear Stallone as Solo saying, "Yeah, I got your Jabba the Hut *right here!*" And the theme song "Gonna Fly Now" would take on a whole new connotation entirely.

Stallone also has famously mentioned the struggle that it took to bring *Rocky* to the big screen. He was turned down by virtually every major Hollywood studio, yet he not only still believed in his script, but also that he should play the lead character. As he tells it, it took ten years to finally get his most famous film made. He saw what others didn't see. His self-concept and understanding of who he was and how he saw himself was ultimately what helped to make his career. As Stallone also has said, "You have to be yourself and do what you know. That's who you have to be."

A great and awesome quote from the movie *Rocky Balboa* *(Rocky 6)*, when Rocky is speaking to his son about his value says, "Now, if you know what you're worth, go out and get what you are worth. But you got to be willing to take the hit, and not point fingers saying you ain't what you want to be because of him, or her, or anybody. Cowards do that and that ain't you. You're better than that!"[3]

In the entire universe, in all time, you are the only you.

Never before have molecules come together exactly like you.

Never again will your footsteps be repeated upon this earth.

No one will ever leave the imprint that you will.

Your strength is a strength someone can count on.

Your love is a love that can make a difference.

Your life is a life that can move the whole world for the better.

Do you dare to make the difference that only you can make? Say, "Yes." You don't go to a gym to *find* a muscle; you go to a gym to *develop* a muscle! There are not any nobodies in this world. God created us all as somebodies. The difference is some people have not yet realized they are somebody!

Listen to the inner voice that tells you that *you matter*; you are smart, important, and awesome. Your name tag should read, "Hello, my name is *I Matter* because I am *somebody*!" Your hash tag reads, "#youmatter10!" On the scale of 1 to 10 you were born a 10, a *somebody*!

Chapter 2

IT HAPPENS!

••• ——————— •••

P ain is inevitable" is a great description of our lives. We all
have experienced many levels of emotional and physical
pain. Somewhere or sometime in life, everyone has been
wounded and hurt in some way. You have either experienced
pain in the past, are experiencing pain now, or *will* experience
pain in the future. A broken heart has been experienced by all
on many occasions; everyone has lost someone or something.
We react out of hurt and pain. From pain comes fear, which
then exemplifies shame and anger. In order to be able to deal
with our pain and eventually conquer it we must first understand what causes it. Where does *it* come from?

There are several types of pain: physical and those that are
considered to be mental, emotional, or psychological in nature.
Many types of pain are known to have their roots in the phys-
iology of the body but are felt more generally as mood-related.
Depression, anxiety, post-traumatic stress, grief, and others

may cause their sufferers as much pain as physical pain does, but are far more difficult to describe or measure since their symptoms are often observed as behavioral. Pain can be acute or chronic. The difference isn't in the way it is defined, but rather in the way it is treated. Too often we treat the symptoms instead of the cause of the pain!

So how do we measure pain? Measurement of pain itself is highly subjective. It varies from person to person. Some may say that women have a higher tolerance for pain because they go through childbirth. Some may say that men have a higher tolerance for pain, because, as in sports, they can often play through it. Many men will just try to "walk it off" and continue competing even though they are hurting. Unlike many other symptoms for which physical tests exist that have definitive answers, pain, whether it is physical or emotional/psychological, can exist in the patient's mind and must be self-reported. There are dozens of scales used to rate pain. This is experienced by patients when the doctor says, "On a scale of 1 to 10, with 10 being the worst, how much does it hurt?" The problem, of course, is that what you report as an 8 may be what someone else would call a 5. That means the scale can only be useful relative to the last answer you gave, or the next answer you give, and not relative to someone else's pain rating. Just as we would grab a coat or run to shelter when a rainstorm or snowstorm threatens us, we need to grab an "emotional overcoat" or a "mental shelter" to run to. The rain, snow, hail, or even wind are viewed by most of us as negative forces that we have to contend with. However, there is a positive outcome to the experience of such tormenting weather: We get motivated to do something to protect ourselves! If we don't, it will overtake us, and we will suffer the consequences. This is often termed "self-preservation."

There is an old saying, "There's a positive for every negative." Honestly, I read so much I cannot remember at this moment whether I learned that in my first grade class or in general life experiences. Where I heard it first doesn't really matter much, but it's the fact that I remembered it. I hope you remember it too! "There's a positive for every negative." Yes, things may look bleak, dark, and very difficult. There are always hope, light, and strength to overcome it. The sun will come up at some point. It will come out tomorrow and always rises to let its light shine bright.

Torrid weather compels us to move to shelter or at least search for covering of some type, whether it's a coat, an umbrella, or a goofy floppy rain hat—and that is how we should view negatives in our emotional and mental lives. Pain can feel unbearable; it can also multiply quickly. We tend to dwell on anything bad that happens to us, no matter how short-lived it is, and we often do nothing to counteract it! It seems to paralyze our minds and bodies, and then begins to erupt into a full-blown depression if we allow it to do so.

Some of us do push it to the side and try not to think about it—and yes, that is one form of action. But just because you are ignoring it does not make it go away. Just because it's out of your sight does not mean that it's not there. It is somewhere lurking.

Unfortunately, the pain often rears its ugly head later on—often in another form that causes us to react with panic, anger, and confusion, simply because we didn't take care of the prior pain. Therefore, we don't know how to deal with the current pain. Two slaps in the face is more than we can take!

Now, we have two negatives which, according to one of the laws of algebra (I do remember!) should equal a positive.... but this is not usually the case when dealing with human energy. Before we realize it, we are actually complaining and whining—if only to ourselves—about our "bad luck." We end up asking ourselves, "Why do these things always happen to *me*?" as if we are the only one that this "bad luck" happens to! When bad things happen, we tend to take it personally. It hits us like a sledgehammer, as if we were the only one experiencing it.

You have to try and stay positive. We've all heard the saying, "Try to look for the good in every situation," and while you try your best to do that, admittedly, it is very difficult sometimes. There have been occasions when you want to scream, cry, throw things, or have a temper tantrum like a little child. In short, you want to act immature, be unreasonable, and "be a crybaby." I think that is natural in all of us at times. We want to revert back to a time when someone else took care of our problems for us. We want someone else to make the decisions, be in charge, and take over the situation. We hear people say, "She's acting childish!" when someone throws a fit, and we think, "I've never done that in my entire adult life." Good for you if you haven't.

What if I have conflicting opinions? Whatever conclusions you come to, they should be right for you. You don't need to feel guilty as long as you aren't hurting someone else. If others give you their opinion, saying that it's not "right," tell them it is perfect for you and they are not you, so they can't possibly realize how you came to this position. Even if they were in the exact same situation as you, they are bringing different viewpoints, pasts, and pains to it, so they still may not react as you are! (That is another fact of life!)

The storms of life will come against you. In any case, "bad weather" got you where you are, but it also helped you to move! It helped you to think of what you should do, and it caused you to take action in one way or another. Now that you've arrived at your emotional shelter, put that coat on, or raised that umbrella over your head, go inside and shut the door on the past! Keep the "bad weather" outside where it belongs! Look around you and notice the beautiful interior of this "shelter"! You can rearrange the furnishings any way you want! It's not only comfortable, but it also protects you, and it will be with you always!

If bad weather comes around again, or if a scary intruder knocks on your door, simply tell them (mentally or verbally) that this is your space, and you will not allow them to enter! Take any further action you need to keep them out, all the while knowing that you are in control of your life! One more thing: if you accidentally leave a window open and the "negatives" start to come in anyway, get out your big guns and take aim!

To avoid pain, many people limit the number of things they do in a day. Eventually, this causes weakness, which leads to even less activity, and a cycle is formed.

While chronic pain is not all in your head, your psychological state plays a huge role in the effect it has on your life. If you or someone you know has chronic pain, you may notice irritability, anger, depression, and difficulty concentrating. The psychological side effects of living with chronic pain can be as debilitating as the pain itself. This is what makes chronic pain such a complex condition.

Emotional pain is the worst kind of pain and the most difficult to deal with. Usually one carries this kind of pain in their subconscious mind if it happened earlier in one's life. Physical and mental abuse as a child can carry into your adult life. When you get some very good counseling, evidence is manifested in your self-confidence and ability to deal with others. In this world we—and *all* who live in it—have some form of dysfunction. We all operate in some level of it. From an early age we experienced our first wound, hurt, and pain. Pain has a message. What's wrong with me? Why did this evil happen? God doesn't love me. I deserve this because I am an evil person. This always happens to me! I am not good enough; I can't and don't measure up! Out of pain comes fear. My desire is that you learn that fear is never your friend! Fear manifests the overwhelming thoughts and feelings of insecurity and inferiority. Our actions become fear-driven, not faith-, hope-, and love-directed. If fear is our motivator, shame and anger display their ugly side. We view who we are by whether we have allowed this pain to label us or not. Our vision becomes skewed through the eyes of pain. The greatest fear we all end up battling is the fear of rejection: "Everyone is better than me, smarter than me, more talented, or prettier than me," and thoughts of that nature. You say to yourself, "I don't deserve good things." Rejection then brings about a lack of trust: trust for others because they have disappointed and hurt us, and trust for ourselves because *we* have failed before!

Our soul, which is made up of our mind, will, and emotions, is constantly seeking what it takes to find relief. Too often we follow the "band-aid perspective." Cover the wound but not go after the true healing of the wound. Scars are not ugly! They are beautiful because they represent a wound that has healed. My focus is that there are still many people walking around with open, gaping wounds on their soul. That's the *why* behind the *whats*! We know the cause! Identifying the cause of why we make some of the negative choices we do is vital. Once we begin to understand the cause, reversing the problem becomes easier. Most people don't relate their actions back to a wound or broken heart they have suffered. That broken heart screams out rejection—what I call "tag your *it*"—to the individual. It's not the game we played as kids, although we could learn something from that game. In life, by tagging your *it*, you identify the "whys" behind the "whats"! The *it* is the source of your pain! The better a doctor understands the cause of an illness, the better and more focused the treatment!

People don't run to abuse, codependency, or addiction because they have nothing better to do. They have spent so much time, money, and effort trying to treat symptoms instead of root problems; they are trying to find relief with a temporary solution. Our soul, which is made up of our mind, will, and emotions, is constantly seeking what it takes to find a solution and relief. Everyone wants to and should feel better about themselves, their circumstances, and their lives! When we understand the *it* that has hurt us, we can then realize the healing for it.

"Unwritten" is an amazing song that debuted in 2004 by British singer and songwriter Natasha Bedingfield. Still, years later, words from this song are impacting the world. Her words are screaming out, knowing what you have experienced up to this point does not have to affect the rest of your life. The rest of your life is still unwritten! The following lyrics from her song shows that. I love the lyrics, "I am unwritten, can't read my mind, I'm undefined, I am just beginning, the pen's in my hand, ending unplanned."[1]

I love the line, "I'm undefined!" In other words, I am not going to let anyone put a definition or label on me anymore! Her song continues: "Staring at the blank page before you, open up the dirty window, let the sun illuminate the words that you could not find..."[2] She is telling us, by describing the dirty window, not to let the pain of the past (*it*) control how we see ourselves, our lives, and our futures. People don't want to be reminded of the wrong they've done; they want to be picked up and loved! Your problem is not permanent. There is an answer. As we identify and know the cause, we have a better chance of implementing some of the positive solutions. The following revelation is one of the greatest epiphanies, or "God winks," to have come to me. "Fear is the result, byproduct, outcome, or manifestation of a lie we have believed. The sooner we can identify that lie, the sooner we can realize God's truth."

Chapter 3

LEAVING YOUR *IT* BEHIND!

••• ──────────── •••

P ain is inevitable, but suffering is optional. It's not how hard you fall but how you get back up. Through my experience, the greatest challenge that faces people is having the desire and ability to let go of their past. Leave your past behind! We determine how much we allow *it* to control and dominate our lives. As we discussed in the last chapter, everyone has an *it*! Since we have all experienced the pain of this world, the best way for you to overcome that pain is to identify your *it*! The key is how we *respond* to our *it*! We either allow ourselves to control *it* or let *it* control us. The simple analogy of letting go can be compared to driving a car. You don't spend most of your time driving looking in the rearview mirror. You can glance back, but the proper way to drive is to spend most of your time looking through the windshield. That's why the windshield is larger than the rearview mirror. Spend most of your time looking in the present on the way to where you are going.

Spending too much time looking in the rearview mirror (your past) will cause you to crash. Life works the same way! When unforgiveness rules your life, it is like participating in a game or an athletic contest that you have planned and prepared to lose! Offenses are inevitable, but forgiveness is optional. The key is our willingness to *forgive* and move forward. It is the greatest choice we can make. When we don't forgive, we relive the pain every moment of every day. Can you forgive me? Can I forgive you? Can we forgive ourselves? I see it this way: inside, we all have a built-in GPS (Global Positioning System) just like many new cars do. As we activate and allow our inner man to flow outward, we gain the strength to do all things. When we do something wrong, or others perpetrate a wrong against us, the built-in GPS within us seems to scream out *recalculate*! In one moment, forgiveness and leaving the hurt behind can heal a family, marriage, relationship, and a career! It is the miracle we all need. The willingness to forgive does not condone wrong; it sets you free! The greatest gift you will ever give yourself is the forgiveness you grant for others and also for yourself! Turn your past hurt into helping others. Give first, and good will return to you. It's the Law of Reciprocity: doing good will return good. Don't practice the Law of Negative Reciprocity: repay evil with evil. That's no way to live. To gain a friend, you need to be a friend. Repay kindness with kindness.

There are no conditions to forgiveness, such as "I will forgive if…when…or but." It's time to get rid of your big *but*. When we don't forgive, we put ourselves in an emotional prison. Compare that to running a race with a person on your back. They are occupying space in your thoughts, feelings, and emotions. Your soul becomes tormented with their presence! You give the person who hurt you permission to continually hurt you—every second, minute, or hour of your life. You allow the past to stay alive and active in *the present*. It would be the same as walking down the aisle to be married while having a U-Haul attached to you. This U-Haul has all your *its* inside. Every hurt and pain that has not been addressed is being brought into this relationship. I don't want to carry past pains for the rest of my life. It's like drinking poison and hoping the person that offended is hurt from the poison *you* drink!

A man was walking on the beach with his wife. He looked up at a beautiful seagull flying overhead. All of sudden, the seagull pooped on his face. He was upset and continually yelled at the seagull to come back and *wipe* the poop off his face. The seagull was laughing as he flew away. The man waited for the seagull to come back and make it right. *It ain't happening!* We can't always control what happens to us or how others treat us. We are in control of our response or reaction to what has happened. You are a victor, not a victim! My problem is based on my attitude. Let's magnify good over the bad!

Love is what we want to be shown in life. I heard three amazing definitions of love: love is not easily offended; love keeps no record of wrong; and lastly, love wants the best for all, doing good to those who have mistreated you. Loving your enemies can describe this one.

When someone hurts you, you may hold on to that anger, resentment, and thoughts of revenge and retribution—or embrace forgiveness and move forward with your life.

Almost everyone has been hurt by the actions or words of another person. The old saying we learned as children, "Sticks and stones may break my bones, but names can never hurt me," is not true. Words are hurtful. They can cut us deeply and have lasting negative effects. Perhaps your mother criticized you as a child, or later she made negative comments about your parenting skills. Perhaps your coworker sabotaged a project you worked very hard on. Or perhaps your partner, spouse, or significant other had a romantic affair. These wounds can leave you with very deep and lasting feelings of anger, bitterness, or even vengeance, but if you don't practice forgiveness, you might be the one who pays most dearly. By embracing forgiveness, you are also able to embrace love, peace, hope, gratitude, and joy.

Practicing forgiveness can lead you down the path to physical, mental, emotional, and spiritual health and well-being. Forgiveness is a conscious decision to let go of resentment and revenge. The hurtful act that offended you might always remain some part of your life, but forgiveness can lessen its grip on you and help you focus on the positive parts of your life rather than the negative. Forgiveness can even lead to feelings of understanding, empathy, and compassion for the person who offended or hurt you.

Forgiveness doesn't mean that you deny the other person's responsibility for offending or hurting you, and it doesn't minimize or justify the wrong that they committed against you. You can forgive the person without condoning the act. Forgiveness brings a peace that helps you go on with life. It frees you from being bound in unforgiveness. One example that I've used to illustrate this is by having two people grab and hold on tightly to one of my arms. I tell the audience that each person who is holding each arm is representing someone who has hurt me or offended me in some way. Their offense has stuck to me, and I carry it with me everywhere I go. Then I walk around with them still holding on tightly as I walk. I explain to the audience that as long as I hold on to that offense, it's like that person is literally latched onto me everywhere I am every day. They may not even have realized that they have hurt me, but

27

as long as I hold that offense inside I am bound by it and drag it with me always. It's a heavy weight that holds me back. I continue to walk and pull them with me across the stage or up and down the aisle for thirty seconds to a minute. By physically seeing the "baggage and bondage" that we carry while holding on to unforgiven offenses, it becomes clear to those who see it. Then I finish the illustration by saying that the only way we can free ourselves from dragging around the heavy bondage (people holding tightly to each arm) is to make a conscious choice to forgive. Then I turn to the person holding on to my right arm and say, "I forgive you." He then releases his grip on my arm. I then turn to the person on my left who is holding tightly to that arm and say, "I forgive you." She also releases her grip. Then I'm totally free and move around the stage or walk through the aisles unbound and with "no baggage" attached. I am free. It was a choice and action that I made. I chose to forgive each of them. That's what set me free.

Letting go of grudges and bitterness can make way for compassion, kindness, and peace. Forgiveness can lead to:

- Healthier and more fulfilling relationships
- Greater spiritual and psychological well-being
- Less anxiety, stress, and hostility
- Lower blood pressure

- Fewer symptoms of depression
- Lower risk of alcohol and substance abuse

When you're hurt by someone—especially by someone you love and trust, you might become angry, sad, or confused. If you dwell on hurtful events or situations, grudges filled with resentment, vengeance, and hostility can grab hold of you and take root in your life. If you allow negative feelings to replace positive feelings, you might find yourself swallowed up by your own bitterness or sense of injustice.

If you're unforgiving, you might pay the price repeatedly by bringing anger and bitterness into every relationship and new experience you have. This is called emotional baggage. Your life can become so wrapped up in the wrong that was committed against you that you can't enjoy the present. It not only holds you back, but it also enslaves you, and you become a prisoner to it. You might become depressed or anxious. You might feel that your life lacks meaning or purpose, or that you're at odds with your personal spiritual beliefs. You might lose valuable and enriching connectedness with others. Connectedness with other people is where we find meaning. Meaning is connectedness. When we share meaning, we connect. All of our lives we are trying to connect with other people. We find happiness in sharing meaning. It's a deep concept, but it's an invaluable concept to understand.

Forgiveness is a commitment to a process of change. To begin, you might:

- Consider the value of forgiveness and its importance in your life at a given time.
- Reflect on the facts of the situation, how you've reacted, and how this combination has affected your life, health, and well-being.
- When you're ready, actively choose to forgive the person who has offended you.
- Move away from your role as victim, and release the control and power the offending person or situation has had in your life.

As you let go of grudges, you'll no longer define your life by how you've been hurt. You won't walk around in a mental state of being the victim. You may even find compassion and understanding.

Forgiveness can be very challenging, especially if the person who has hurt you doesn't know or admit wrong, or doesn't speak of or show sorrow for hurting you in the first place. If you find yourself stuck, consider the situation from the other person's point of view. Ask yourself why he or she would behave in such a way. Usually the reason that someone has hurt you is because they themselves have been hurt or emotionally wounded in some way. Behavior is learned and passed down—sometimes from generation to generation. Children learn what they see and experience, and then, as adults, they emulate that behavior. Perhaps you would have reacted similarly if you faced the same background or life situation they have lived through. This is not condoning their behavior but could help us to understand why they did it. In addition, consider broadening your view of the world. Expect occasional imperfections from the people in your life. You might want to reflect on times you've hurt others and on those who've forgiven you. It can also be helpful to write in a journal, pray, use guided meditation, or talk with a person you've found to be wise, trustworthy, and compassionate, such as a spiritual leader, a mental health provider, or an impartial loved one or friend.

If the hurtful event involved someone whose relationship you otherwise value, forgiveness can lead to reconciliation. This isn't always the case, however. Reconciliation might be impossible if the offender has died or is unwilling to communicate with you. In other cases, reconciliation might not be appropriate. Still, forgiveness is always possible, even if reconciliation isn't. It's a choice you make. It's an action you take. Forgive or not forgive, that is the question.

If you haven't reached a state of forgiveness, being near someone who has hurt you might be very stressful. To help handle these situations or alleviate this tension, remember that you can choose to attend or avoid specific functions and gatherings. Why put yourself in stressful situations when you have the power and choice to do so or not? Respect yourself, and do what seems best. If you choose to be around those people who have offended you, don't be surprised by a certain amount of tension, awkwardness, and perhaps even more intense feelings. Do your best to keep an open mind and heart in the situation. You might find that the experience helps you to move forward with or toward genuine forgiveness.

Some people think that holding a grudge against another is a way to control the other person and get back at them. Getting another person to change his or her actions, behavior, or words isn't the point of forgiveness. Think of forgiveness more about how it can change your life—by bringing you peace, happiness, and emotional and spiritual healing. By having and embracing unforgiveness, you are actually allowing the other person to dictate or hold power over you. Forgiveness can completely take away the power the other person continues to wield in your life.

The first step is to honestly assess and acknowledge the wrongs you've done and how those wrongs have affected others' lives. At the same time, try to avoid judging yourself too harshly. You're human, and you make mistakes. You will hurt others, sometimes intentionally, but also unintentionally. If you're truly sorry for something you've said or done, consider admitting it to those you've harmed. Humbly taking responsibility is not easy to do, but the mere act of genuine humility is very powerful in itself. Speak of your sincere sorrow or regret, and specifically ask for forgiveness—without making excuses. Remember, however, you can't force someone to forgive you. Others need to move to and grant forgiveness in their own time. Whatever the outcome may be, commit to treating others with sincere compassion, empathy, and genuine respect.

To recover from conflict management failures, one must understand and forgive. Forgiveness is a communication process that allows you and your partner to overcome the damage done to your relationship because of a transgression.

Forgiveness has several steps: Confession occurs when the offending person acknowledges wrongdoing, Venting is verbally and nonverbally expressing emotions. Understanding occurs when partners express what motivated the transgression. An apology is a direct verbal message that acknowledges responsibility, expresses regret or remorse, and directly requests forgiveness. Forgiving explicitly or implicitly communicates to our partners that we absolve them from the consequences or penalties we have a right to impose. Part of forgiveness is to re-establish the rules or set new rules. Partners should monitor the relationship as they move past the incident.

Expressions I heard growing up were: "Two wrongs don't make a right," and "You can't fight fire with fire. Adding fire to fire makes the burn greater." Forgiveness is the *water* that puts out the fire that has attacked you.

The need to forgive is widely recognized by the public, but they are often at a loss for ways to accomplish it. For example, in a large representative sampling of American people on various religious topics in 1988, the Gallup Organization found that 94 percent said it was important to forgive, but 85 percent said they needed some outside help to be able to forgive.[1] However, not even regular prayer was found to be effective. Related to forgiveness is the concept of mercy, so even if a person is not able to complete the forgiveness process he or she can still show mercy, especially when so many wrongs are done out of weakness rather than malice. The Gallup poll revealed that many people found the only thing that was effective for them was "meditative prayer."[2] Finding support groups and ways to begin the forgiveness process is vital.

Forgiveness wants the best for the person who wounded you and to not condone the wrong. Remember, they treated you wrongly because their *it* had never been left behind! Don't allow a wound to label and identify you! Your wound tells you that you don't matter; your fingerprints say *you matter*! You want them to be blessed and to succeed the way you want to succeed. Kathy Sanders lost two grandchildren in the Oklahoma City Bombing. During the trial she befriended Terry Nichols's mom. He was the mastermind behind the bombing. She knew that his mom was devastated and hurting. By being kind and loving to his mom she brought total healing into her own life.[3] I believe if we operate in *true* love, we won't have to forgive. *True* love never takes offense in the first place, so forgiveness is not needed. Let this be the goal you shoot for: don't take offense, and leave your *it* behind!

Many of you may not know my own personal story. I could not control a doubly legally drunk driver from crashing through my house, killing my wife, and seriously injuring me. I could only control what I can control, which is how I respond. The ancient Greek philosopher Epectitus says it so clearly, "It's not what happens to you, it's what you do about it"![4] My willingness to forgive set me free! I know the good Lord gives us the strength to do the right thing. Three and half years later I was married again to a beautiful woman from Mineola, Long Island, New York. In May 1989, Suzanne Marie Nick and I joined in holy matrimony. I now have been married for over twenty-five years with two amazing sons, Alec and Aron. I have traveled this world sharing hope with millions. The greatest lesson I can teach my children is to leave your *it* behind! I have had the honor of authoring and co-authoring seventeen different books. My willingness to forgive from my heart has allowed me to triumph over tragedy!

Free your pain! Slow down, and embrace the journey. Participate in your own learning and healing. How do we forgive? We choose to, one decision at a time. One conscious choice and moment at a time! Choose from the power within, not from the outside influences. I choose how I see. Be able to say, "I will not be defined by others or by what has happened to me." When the past rules my life, it hinders me from being and doing what I have been placed on this earth to accomplish. I can only control how I respond. Allow it to take place in your heart. When we bully a bully; we stoop to their level. One of the greatest lines ever spoken was by Rafiki in Disney's *Lion King* movie. "Oh yes, the past can hurt. But from the way I see it, you can either run from it...or learn from it."[5] Every time you head down that road of the past, your inner GPS is screaming out, "Recalculate!" Take the weapon out of their hands moment by moment! I call it, "Ten seconds at a time." I can do anything good or right for ten seconds. Keep adding the ten seconds up, and you eventually have one minute, one hour, one day, one week, one month, one year, and one lifetime! It's never too late to recalculate! It's time to *leave* your past behind!

Chapter 4

TURN PAIN TO PURPOSE

··· —————————— ···

I believe that *God* put dreams into our hearts. Our job in life, according to God, is to make those dreams reality despite anyone's criticism of us. You may be creative. You may be an inventor. You've had ideas and dreams of different machines running through your mind since you were six years old. Only now (I'm over thirty-five) do I truly understand what it is God wanted me to do with my life. You may be going through life trying to live as normal (whatever that is) a life as you can. You'll eventually marry, have two kids, and a good income, but it's not enough. You need to feel that "average" isn't enough. You need to feel that your family deserves better. You need to listen to God's voice. He will fulfill your dreams.

I believe we have the power to turn our pain into purpose. As we discussed, forgiveness is vital. As we move through our pain, we can bring hope to others who are living through it. Helping others overcome is awesome. It is the greatest success. In life we all either have experienced, are experiencing, or will experience pain. The common bond we have is that pain is inevitable. We may not be able to relate to circumstances, but we can relate to the pain. When I worked with surviving family members of 9-11, I couldn't relate to their situation, but I could relate to loss and its specific kind of pain. We connected over having someone ripped out of our lives.

Why do bad things happen to good people? That's one of the mysteries of life. It is true that bad things happen to everyone at some point. That is a harsh fact of life, and there is no getting around it. But to focus on bad things in our lives means that we believe that life is bad! Life is not bad! Turn that negative thinking around, and start to believe that life is good with the occasional "bad thing" occurring at very random and infrequent times! Sometimes it's good to reflect and think about your life. If you look at the entire span of your life—or even a mere 1-year period in your life—how much time did bad things take up? How often did they really happen? Was it 75 percent of the time? Was it 50 percent of the time? Was it 25 percent of the time? Was it 10 percent of the time? Was it less than 5 percent of the time? If we look at life realistically, we see that "bad things" occur much more infrequently than our minds and hearts believe they do! In actuality, unless you are consistently making poor or ignorant decisions, you will find that "bad things" happen 1 percent or less of the total time of our lives.

Physical pain and emotional pain are different things. When bad things happen, emotional pain can be very hard to bear, but it must be borne. There is no medicine available except the ones that put you to sleep, and then you pass the time without even knowing it. Try to understand that, when something is bothering you so badly that you feel emotional pain, it is a sign that you have not yet come to terms with the matter, and eventually you will need to. So you might as well start trying to accept it right now! Emotional pain is in the mind, and if we can control it, then we can stop it. Think about what is causing you pain, and try to think of positive things that will eventually come from it.

Some of the things to do for emotional pain are: pray, read, draw, paint, sculpt, go to a park and take a walk, or sometimes just cry till you can't cry anymore and then sleep it off. As I just mentioned, sometimes it helps to talk to someone or just to keep a journal and write about what's troubling you. Sometimes it's good to see a therapist or counselor to get you through the rough spots. Hang in there! Things *will* get better. Knowing it will get better helps the most. The pain does not last forever. Sooner or later you can find a way to deal with it in a constructive way and feel better about it. Talking it out helps mostly because I have friends who help me to eventually come to a point where I can laugh about it—especially the embarrassing, heart wrenching stuff.

How can I cope with chronic pain in my life? While you may see a grim picture when you think of living with chronic pain, keep in mind that these are worst-case scenarios. In reality, many people continue to live healthy, productive lives in spite of their pain. This is because they have found ways to cope with the pain, either through medications, alternative treatments, or a combination of the two. If you suffer from chronic pain, here are some additional tips for getting your life back.

The best way to deal with emotional pain which you most likely received from another is to surround yourself with people who really care about you. In times of difficulty, you will know who your true friends and loved ones are. They will stick with you no matter what. They will drop everything to be there for you. Surrounding yourself with loved ones will put your mind to ease because you are wrapped up in being happy with the ones who are there for you. It will help lift your spirit and give you the positive support you need.

It's okay to vent your anger. It's okay to get upset. Being able to do so is part of the healing process. Granted, there are times when it is not "appropriate" to act like this—at least according to society's rules of conformity—but everyone has had their moments of insecurity and have acted as inappropriately as you have at one time or another. It happens; get over it. It may just be the release you need in order to begin anew. Scream, yell, jump up and down, punch a punching bag, hit a tennis ball, kick a soccer ball around a field—whatever it takes, just do it in a positive way and get that negative energy out of your body and you will feel much better.

One of the best techniques I have found is music. After Ava was killed I could lose myself in it and completely forget about the pain. I prefer uplifting, spiritual music (yes, I'm referring to Christian music) because that is what I most enjoy. It calms me and is quite soothing. However, there are times when I need to get my butt moving and accomplish things beyond my normal routine, so I pull out the big guns. Would you believe, at these moments, I power through the pain and pick up speed by listening to country music? It's true, and that's a little secret. Music can be a great source of coping with pain. But you need to be careful that it has a positive effect on you and your behavior. Lyrics matter. Anyone who says that lyrics don't matter is crazy. I hear people in public singing, rapping, or quoting aloud the latest lyrics to songs and in addition to the fact that every other word is either a curse word or degrading in some way—it's definitely not positive or uplifting in any way.

Meditation is very useful, as is prayer. Some people use massage or biofeedback—whatever works for you. Even scented candles, especially lavender, can soothe. I don't know what chemical properties lavender holds, but many people have found a lavender-scented product used at bedtime greatly improves their sleep.

It's an old saying that "laughter is the best medicine," and it's true. Comedies, humorous books, etc.—one can never laugh too much, too long, or too often. One great way to cope with pain is through laughter. After Ava, my first wife, was killed by a drunk driver, many times to deal with her loss I would laugh repeatedly to old episodes of *The Three Stooges*. I loved it, and I needed it. Comedy was part of my remedy for dealing with my pain. It was great medicine.

The next positive step would be to take a deep breath, step back, and think of your options. What can you do to rid yourself of this pain and forgive those who inflicted it on you? Remember, the "person who hurt you" may even be yourself, so it may be doubly-hard to grant forgiveness in that case, but it is possible! Many times the hardest person to forgive is yourself.

What else can you do to deal with pain? Learn to identify stress triggers. What upsets you? Is there any way you can avoid it, or allow it to affect you less? Sometimes just being aware of what increases your stress and pain levels can help keep things under control. Try keeping a pain journal. Talk to someone. Find support groups. Discuss your feelings with your doctor. Tell your family and friends how you are coping. Keeping everything inside allows stress to build up, leading to more pain and an increased risk for depression. Try a different medication. Medications work differently for many people. Sometimes a medication may simply stop working for you. If you find your prescription is no longer effective in treating your pain or your depression, don't be afraid to ask your doctor for a change. Do as much as you can. Even when you are having a bad day, it is important to keep a steady level of activity. Allowing pain to interfere with your daily routine puts you at risk for losing endurance. It also increases feelings of helplessness, a factor that contributes to depression. Relax. Find outlets for stress wherever possible. Read a book, take a bath, or find a quiet place to sit for a few minutes. Keep stress levels in check by taking a time out when you need it.

Finding ways to deal with stress and cope with chronic pain can give you a head start in the battle against depression. Unfortunately, both depression and chronic pain come with a stigma that keeps some people from seeking the treatment they need. Even though these conditions may be uncomfortable to talk about, keeping them in the open is the best way to keep them in check.

Exercise can help with alleviating chronic pain. My friend's grandmother used to tell him, "If you don't lose it; use it. And if you don't use it, you'll lose it." Talk to your doctor or a physical therapist about a safe exercise program that is right for you. When you live with chronic pain, exercise helps you maintain your mobility. It also keeps your muscles active and your joints flexible, which alleviates the symptoms of chronic pain.

Regular exercise also prevents something called disuse syndrome, a condition in which muscles become weak from inactivity. Weak muscles are more vulnerable to pain and can even cause other injuries. They begin to atrophy from non-use.

You may want to use some alternative treatments. Used alone or combined with medications, complementary and alternative treatments (CAMs) can be a powerful tool in learning to live with chronic pain. Some examples of commonly used CAMs for chronic pain are massage, magnetic therapy, energy medicine, acupuncture, and herbal medicine.

Everyone needs to try to relax. Stress causes muscle tension, which can increase the amount of pain you feel. When you allow your muscles to relax you will experience reduced strain and decreased pain sensations. Learning to relax your body can help you control your pain without the use of additional medications. Relaxation is a pain management tool that can be used on its own or in combination with other treatments.

Yoga and guided imagery are useful in decreasing stress and muscle tension—major contributors to the intensity of chronic pain. Yoga uses a series of poses combined with deep breathing to relax your mind and your body. Guided imagery uses meditation to calm your mental state.

Emotional pain is always hard to control. The difference between feeling better or feeling pity for yourself is sometimes a moment of relief that makes you stronger to endure your sufferings. No recipe is perfect for everyone; you have to find it for times when you are alone, every day, and combined with your different moods. Practice and experience are the only ways to give you more certain ways to feel better. You *can* be strong. Nothing lasts forever! God doesn't simply renovate, rehabilitate, or restore the past. He makes all things new! Don't give power to your pain. Turn your pain into purpose! Remember, *you matter*! *It* doesn't.

Chapter 5

I WANT YOU TO SHOW ME!

••• ———————— •••

I mentioned in an early chapter about my favorite song anthem. The band named Foreigner rocked it out in the 70s and 80s and capped it off as lead vocalist Lou Gramm sang, "I want to know what love is, I want you to show me!"[1] Love *matters* because *love* changes everything. Yes, we *all* desire to be shown what love is. What love looks like, and how it feels to love and be loved. Relationships are based on this simple fact—showing love and being shown love! When you realize how much other people matter as much as *you matter*, then it's easier to treat others the way you want to be treated, valued, and esteemed. When people love themselves, they are able to love others. Love and purpose always heals the heart—not just the hearts of others, but *our* hearts also! Evil is present when people refuse to love.

You can never get close to or bond with someone you are afraid of. People want to feel important and valued. They will run to whomever or wherever they feel safe. Safety is a primary need that all of us want to have—people as well as animals. Let's consider how a dog reacts. When a dog feels scared or afraid, it will approach you in one of two ways: it will either come toward you cautiously with its head down and sometimes even visibly shaking, or it will approach you with a menacing growl and showing its fanged teeth or barking in an angry attack mode—definitely not wagging its tail! But when dogs are loved and excited to see you, their whole demeanor is different. When they approach you, their tails wag out of control, back and forth at a million miles per hour in happiness, and their tongues slobber, panting in glee.

MY *IT*

I had an uncle Tony. Yes, we were very creative with our name choices. I remember as a kid he would talk about his time during WWII. I always was interested in what he did there, but all he ever said was that he was a coward and flew small planes that delivered supplies to the allies. However, he was so afraid that he would at times drop the supplies behind enemy lines so he could make it back to base safely. I'm not sure if I believed him or not, but I always pictured Germans wearing American uniforms and eating our rations, thanks to my uncle.

Years later, after some years as a police officer, I asked my uncle again what it was like. He finally sat me down and gave me a glimpse of what atrocities he survived throughout his ordeal as a soldier for this great country. How he and his unit, I believe an engineer unit, found themselves in the middle of the Battle of the Bulge. How the river ran red with blood from both sides and finally how he and the others tore the Airborne patches from the uniforms of the dead and dying Americans and attached them to their own so the Germans would think there was an endless supply of America's best. He said he knew he would die during that battle, but when he found himself alive and victorious, he knew that any day forward was a blessing. Those years of battle defined his life—his defining moment—or his *it* moment. A few weeks before before he died, we spoke again at my dad's house in Florida.

But man... to be able for just a minute to go back and participate in one of those meals... to smell the smells, taste the tastes, laugh the laughs, hug my family, and tell them that I am thankful for them—that they are my defining moment, my *it* moment.

That is exactly what I'm grateful for.

The fundamental key to reaching others, or being reached, is how someone feels about themselves in the presence of others. There has to be a connection. Our need for belonging is our need to connect. One of the greatest lines from such an awesome and inspiring movie *Remember the Titans* was, "Attitude reflects leadership."[2] True leadership is servant leadership. Great leaders know that they are only as good as the people under them. True strength is shown in our willingness to serve. They understand the value of humility and serving those around them. Always wanting and working for the best of others while truly wanting them to be successful. This will automatically bring the best out of a person and the one serving. The goal of a great leader is to help others reach their maximum ability potential. When you are in leadership and you assist in helping others raise their level toward excellence, it's a direct reflection on you because you made it happen with them. We are either about serving others or focusing on others serving us. I share with teachers and coaches all the time about this simple principle. You as a leader may be the only hope given to your protégé. People aren't hopeless; they sometimes just don't have hope. People aren't faithless; they sometimes just don't have faith because of hurt and pain. That's why a great leader is a leader by example. A leader wants to show you the way.

In athletic teams, the players are playing to win, playing not to lose, or playing not to make a mistake. Players always want to feel that they are part of the team—that they are included. I can't understand why a "players' coach" (a coach who relates well and brings out the best in his players) is not the norm. This term is a phrase used by players to describe a coach they love to play for, and oftentimes play very hard for. There is a real connection between the players and the coach. The coach is able to articulate his strategy and motivate his players because they believe in what he is trying to do for the good of the team. It seems like most coaches are not players' coaches! There isn't a strong connection and understanding between the players and coach. Therefore, athletes play with fear and trepidation because they feel they are walking on eggshells. Their response is an athletic performance based on not wanting to make a mistake instead of playing with confidence, taking some risks, and trying to win. They won't "play to win" because they are so caught up and intimidated by how the coach might react to their mistakes.

Personally, this is why I hate shame! Shame doesn't speak to you that you made a mistake. That is guilt. Shame tells you, "You are a mistake"! There are no mistakes—just people who make them. That describes everyone. We all make mistakes. I once heard a story about an arrogant man who boasted that he was "Never, ever wrong!," but finally and jokingly admitted that he was mistaken. These are my words to all who feel shame: "Shame, shame, go away—never come back another day!

This carries over into all fields. Every area of life has someone in a leadership position. What should matter most to a true leader is what matters most to the ones they are leading! Get a life degree in knowing what makes the people you are leading tick! Study them to know their likes and dislikes and what motivated them to action. Passion for others being successful over one's own success is imperative! Some leaders are even caught up in abusive methods. I believe this is fear driven. If the person they are leading doesn't succeed, then they feel it is a reflection on them. The method is not sacred; it is the message of love! True love allows the person being led to have permission to make a mistake. In making a mistake he or she is now comfortable enough to take responsibility and apologize.

People always remember how you made them feel. They may not remember other details regarding the situation or your shared experience, but they will always remember how you made them feel. We make mental notes of how we are treated. Are we treated with dignity and respect? Or disrespected as if we don't matter? When I went through the horrific tragedy of losing my wife Ava, I remember how I felt about myself because of the genuine love of so many who rallied around me to support me. Many friends and family came from all over the country to be by my side. The overwhelming love of all the students and faculty from Santa Fe High School and Middle

School in Santa Fe, Texas, was unforgettable to say the least! I always want them to know how valuable and loved they were and, in fact, still are to me. They responded like a sponge being squeezed. What goes in also goes out. The love they soaked in was so full that it squeezed out on my behalf when I needed it the most. As a former coach I always had my mind set that my third string fullback got in every game. I didn't tell him, "Just stand on the sidelines and cheer!" I actively looked for every opportunity to insert him into the game so he could be a participant, not just a spectator on the sidelines! If only for several plays, he got the call to go into the game. I knew that although he was not first or second string, allowing him to play would encourage him to continually work harder and harder. I didn't have to force him. He knew his coach loved and believed in him. If I told him to run through a wall, he would do it. No questions asked. The athlete who questions you often wonders what your motives are. Is it about them or me? If an athlete has confidence in how I see him, he then knows I wouldn't ask him to do something he didn't have the potential to achieve. I wouldn't do anything to hurt him. When he got into the game for several plays and received praised, he would follow me around like an excited puppy.

The day I buried my Ava, a dangerous tropical storm named Hurricane Juan had moved from the Gulf of Mexico into the

Houston area and drenched us with several inches of rain, high winds, and tornadoes. Even through torrential downpours of rain, over five hundred students from Santa Fe High School and Middle School let their actions speak volumes for how they felt about me. They first filled up the church during the memorial service, then followed me almost twenty-five miles to downtown Houston in the pouring rain all the way to the cemetery. I remember standing by the gravesite with Ava's casket as I said goodbye to her when the officials told us that we had to leave immediately because of the dangerous weather in the immediate area. As I looked up and was about to leave, I could see flooding in the cemetery—not the drenching water that was everywhere—but flooding into the cemetery, with no umbrellas, mud up to their ankles, soaking wet from head to toe, their hairdos all a mess—those five hundred students from Santa Fe High and Middle School rushing toward me like a tidal wave of love ready to wash over me and envelope me. That's a sight I will never forget and often play it over and over in my mind. I wanted to know what love is; they wanted to show me.

While spending twenty-three days in the hospital and having three major surgeries, they never left my side. They were with me 24-7! Twenty-four hours, seven days a week. The kindness, the love, and the bedside manner of the hospital staff was incredibly comforting to me. It's a feeling I've treasured, even years later when I think about it. I don't remember how overwhelming my physical and emotional pain was, but I do remember how loved and cared for I was by so many who showed me what love truly is! Being loved is what I remember most! Gifts are not gifts until they are given away. They are meant to be given, not held on to! The late actor Robin Williams showed this so well when he played the doctor in *Patch Adams*. "Patch" understood the importance of love in his bedside manner and regular interaction with the terminally ill children he treated each day. He did whatever it took to help them feel most loved and comfortable, often times with the gift of laughter. He understood that any method, even those that may not be practical to others can be utilized to bring faith, hope, and love to his sick patients. They remembered how they felt more than the painful diseases they were battling.

Love should have no limits. As a speaker, or being from Brooklyn—a talker, I want to strive to encourage everyone who hears my voice. I know it is crucial how my audience feels about themselves in my presence. Recently I received a phone call from a hospital director in Chico, California. He introduced himself as Alan Weintraub. He was calling me to discuss the potential of me traveling to California to address his hospital staff. During our discussion, Alan said to me, "May I ask you several personal questions?" I said, "Sure. You can ask me anything you'd like." He continued, "Are you the same Bobby Petrocelli who grew up in Sheepshead Bay, Brooklyn?" "Yes," I said. "Did you live on East 24th Street, attend Shell Bank Junior High School, play baseball at Bedford Park, and have an uncle named Rico Petrocelli who played professional baseball for the Boston Red Sox?" My response was, "Yes, yes, yes, and yes, so how do you know me?"

"Bobby, I used to live on East 27th Street, three blocks away from you. I attended the Yeshiva school on Avenue Z. I used to come to Bedford Park all the time. I watched you play baseball, but always from a distance. One year for my birthday, I got a brand-new baseball glove as a present. I was so excited that I came over to Bedford Park. Instead of watching you from a distance, I came closer to the fence than ever before. You noticed me standing outside the fence with my new glove in my hand. Then you asked me my name and if I wanted to play baseball with you and your friends. Wow! You have no idea how long I wanted to play with you guys and what that meant to me that you asked me to play too. I was a die hard Yankee fan and hated the Red Sox. Everyone in the neighborhood knew you as Rico Petrocelli's nephew. The thought of playing baseball with Rico Petrocelli's nephew sent shivers down my spine. But spending the next two hours playing baseball with you and your friends in Bedford Park one sunny afternoon was one of the greatest highlights of my young life!"

There was a momentary pause, then Alan continued by saying, "As we left the park, we headed up East 24th Street to the corner of Avenue Y. You encouraged me to come and play baseball anytime with you and your friends." Back in those days we just showed up at the park or yelled out the window to our friends that we were going to play baseball—that was our communication system. We had rotary dial phones in those days. Ones that we kids were not allow to use, only the grown-ups could. Plus, it took so long to dial somebody's number—by the time the rotary went around for each number, it took two minutes just to dial.

Alan continued, "As I was walking back to my house, I realized I had left my new birthday baseball glove at the park. I came running and crying back to you, Bobby. You encouraged me not to worry and that you would go back to the park and help me find it. When we arrived back at the park, I noticed some older kids had gotten ahold of my glove. Bobby, you and I walked up to them to try and get it back. I approached them and asked them for it. They began to tease me and hit me in the face with my own glove. You stepped in and said to one of the older teens, "Is that your glove? Is your name Alan? My friend's name is Alan! That's his glove that he left here. Either you are going to give him his glove back or I'm gonna get it back for him!" Alan paused again, "I couldn't believe it. That older teen immediately gave me my glove back." We both laughed. Then Alan excitedly said, "From that moment on—I was not only the biggest Bobby Petrocelli fan—but the biggest Yankee fan that now also loved the Boston Red Sox and Rico Petrocelli. We walked back to the corner of East 24th Street and Avenue Y."

"As I turned to say, 'goodbye' and walk home, you said to me, 'Alan, I forgot to tell you…I'm going to my grandma's house in the Catskill Mountains in upstate New York. I won't be back for about a month, but when I come back, let's play baseball together. I'll see you then, all right?' Alan continued, 'As I was walking away, I turned back to wave and say my final goodbye, little did I know that that would be the last time I would ever see you, thirty-five years ago.'"

My jaw dropped as he was telling me this. I had forgotten about this, but now he rekindled my memory. Alan went on to say, "Within two weeks my dad got an immediate job transfer to Southern California. We left before you came back from the Catskills. Bobby, I have never forgotten what you did for me when I was twelve years old. It was truly a defining and life changing moment for me. It was an epiphany! When you got my glove back, you changed my life forever! Bobby, your actions for me screamed out, '*You matter*, Alan!' I'll never forget that."

My son Alec's reaction to two different college football coaches he played for confirms what I have just discussed. While he was a freshman at University of North Carolina-Chapel Hill, his defensive line coach resigned. In Alec's eighteen years, I never saw him so devastated. He absolutely loved Coach B and, more than anything, how he felt about himself when Coach B coached him on the field and further talked to him off the field. Coach B's message through his words and actions toward Alec was simple: "*You matter!*" The coach who followed him as the next defensive line coach resigned to pursue a coaching position at another university. The response of Alec and the rest of the UNC players to the departure of this coach were totally different than their response to Coach B leaving. They were all exuberant that this other coach was leaving. The players didn't even say goodbye to him. My heart broke for this coach. Winning is everything in sports as long as it is not self-serving. Abusing, using, or taking advantage of others is not winning in sports. Life is no different. The feeling of shame they felt around him was evident in how ecstatic they were when he left. Attitude reflects leadership! *The Monkees* song in the 60s spoke it loudly and clearly, "We were born to love one another..."[3]

"I want to know what love is; I want you to show me!" Be the me that shows the love people are searching for. Love the heck out of them. First love them with everything you've got.

If you are going to err, err by loving too much! Secondly, by loving them, you help rid them of the hell that is haunting, hurting, and destroying them. Everyone wants to feel better about who they are. We all have a great desire to be included and not excluded. Everyone feels special when they are remembered. The theme song for the TV sitcom *Cheers* had a verse that said it best: "Where everybody knows your name."[4] Be the one who invites those who normally do not get invited. Jasmine, a high school junior in Washington state, told how painful it was when she sat down at a table in the cafeteria and one of the other students at the table asked, "Who invited you?" She said it broke her heart. Jasmine thanked me after my assembly program for inviting and including everyone. Be defined as a heart above the rest!

Faith, hope, and love are the three qualities I wish for all of you. They are considered the best. Faith is awesome, and hope is necessary, but the greatest of these is *love*! Everyone wants to know what love is! Be the one!

Chapter 6

YOU, ME, WE!

··· —————————— ···

E verybody wants to know that they matter! Having the feeling of importance, value, and love is essential to all of us. *You matter. I matter. We matter*! It's all about the *we*! We base our lives on what we believe we can or cannot do, or what we allow ourselves to become or try to achieve. The fact that we each have distinctly different fingerprints is proof of God's approval in us. Of the billions of people on earth, no two have the exact same fingerprint. No two. Not even twins. My personal faith tells me that God made us all 100 percent unique as well as diverse. If everyone were supposed to be black or white or red or yellow then we are saying, "God, you messed up! Everyone is supposed to look like me and act like me."

If unity was not so essential, then division wouldn't be so prominent. The greatest form of power is through unity, people working together for a common goal. The power of together! To me the most awesome example of this is the mindset of the

Navy Seals. The greatest fear of a Seal member is to *not be there* for their fellow comrades in time of need. They are more fearful of letting down their team members than dying. Wow!

In sports, not everyone can play the same position. Each player has their role on the team. Remember, a quarterback is only as good as the offensive line blocking for him. Even a great running back will be a non-factor in a game if he has no blocking. Each player has a job to do, and the fate of the team rests in how well they play together and carry out their individual roles. You will never have a game winning field goal if the snap is bad or the hold is no good. The kicker will have no chance. Each part of a field goal attempt has to be executed well for it to split the uprights.

One of my favorite childhood cartoons was Bugs Bunny. In one episode Bugs was playing every position on the baseball field at the same time. If Bugs was the pitcher how could he also be the catcher? Could he throw the ball and then also race behind home plate to receive it as well? The episode had him running crazy to cover all the positions. It was very chaotic for Bugs to try to do it all by himself! Life is no different. In unity we can accomplish all things. Everything is possible. *United* we stand, but *divided* we fall! The sad reality is that there are too many people who make a living by stirring up and advancing division among people. They are dividers and opportunists who run to every opportunity they can, even before they know the true details or whole story of what actually happened. They divide us against each other. They don't care about the truth, and things quickly spiral out of control because of their personal agendas. Their actions encourage deviant and immoral behavior.

The prevalence of division in our society is very disturbing. Many times people, because of past hurt, use this as an excuse for bad behavior or false accusations and judgments. It's always easier to blame someone else and feel the right of entitlement to perform a disturbing act. When someone senses injustice, it doesn't give him the right to loot or destroy other people's property. We don't have to agree with all things, but there are much better ways to protest the unfairness. Losing my wife gave me no right to hurt others or destroy other people's property. My hurt and anger doesn't condone wrong behavior. If that is the case, there is something much deeper that is not being looked at.

Recently one of my friends was walking in the city and was approached by a man selling bootleg DVDs on the street. Counterfeiters are now so sophisticated that they can have their illegal movie DVD copies available at the same time that the film is newly released to the general public in theaters. . . . sometimes even before the premiere release. My friend, knowing bootleg DVDs are illegal (not a *Seinfeld* episode about George bootlegging) waved the man off to show that he was not interested in making a purchase. The bootlegger took offense to my friend's rejection of his sales pitch. He believed my friend was not buying a DVD from him only because the bootlegger was from a different racial background—not because my friend believes that bootlegging counterfeit DVDs is illegal! Here's the kicker of how ignorant people are and use utter stupidity as an excuse: My friend actually happens to have an adopted son who is from the exact same racial background as the illegal DVD street salesman! People like the bootlegger need to address their own prejudices and pain before passing unsubstantiated judgment against others!

Can't we all just get along? We are more similar than we are different from one another. Everyone with whom we may disagree and fight has the same desire deep down inside. What is it? To be loved, valued, and to know that *they matter*! The greatest form of affirmation is teamwork affirmation—working together and accomplishing great things. There is no "I" in teamwork. This transcends all races, cultures, and professions. The power of a unified group, all working for the same goal is greater than the individual's efforts! The greater the unity, the greater the ability! I call it the "charcoal briquette theory"! When someone barbecues on a grill using charcoal briquettes, their goal is to reach the best cooking heat temperature as quickly as possible. As an experienced grill master myself, I know that this occurs when all the briquettes are next to each other and on top of each other. This hot coal configuration brings the best heat when each briquette burns with both its own heat and also the heat of the other coal briquettes it is connected to. Now when the coals are spread out, they still maintain their high degree of cooking heat. That simple principal works for us, too. We need to live from within. The pilot light inside each one of us can ignite you to be all that you have been placed on this earth to be. Just as the coals emit the greatest heat after being connected to other hot coals, we can have our own light burn brightest— our own talents shine brightest, even when we are separated from the previous sparks that we formerly were connected to. But it's the connection that helped to optimize us.

Each one of us has been tremendously blessed by those who have given freely to us, so we can, in the same way, bless and freely give to others. Any gift given is never too small. The travesty is not giving your gift away to help others. As the band Red Hot Chili Peppers sang, "Give it away, give it away, and give it away now."[1] Too many people don't realize that the greatest source of power is in serving others. My new friend Garrett from Minnesota and I connected because he has something in common with my younger son. They both play hockey. The difference is that we live in Florida, not normally thought of as a "hockey state." Aron absolutely loves hockey. Garrett and Aron connected through Facebook. After speaking at Garrett's junior high school, he came to talk with me during lunchtime while I was in the school cafeteria. He thanked me for telling him and his school how much *everybody matters*! Garrett is a phenomenal example of working through adversity. He told me, "Bobby, thanks for confirming to me that *I matter*—that I have a great purpose, a great value, and have great importance. I will not allow my bilateral radical aplasia diagnosis to stop me from being all that I am! I haven't. And I will continue to fulfill my destiny. My school principal helped me understand this, and now you, Bobby, have confirmed this to me by your presence and speaking to us this morning."

You matter way too much not to succeed in your life. One thing that we have to understand is that we desperately need each other. The concept of team is one that everyone works to understand and nurture in their own profession or job. A team is a unique group of people coming together for a common purpose or goal. When you observe differences in people, they are evident in a variety of ways. Geographic, racial, socioeconomic, religious, and age differences are unique factors that influence a team's chemistry and ability to work together. Each member has varying levels of experience and maturity. True team players understand what it is to be challenged and how to best face adversity. They are accountable to something greater than themselves individually—the team's success! The power of *we*. Leaders know the importance of working toward inclusion rather than exclusion. Most successful leaders go out of their way to welcome, greet, and say hello to each member every day to encourage inclusion. This is called building rapport. Rapport is the common bond and trust between team members and colleagues working together. Developing a strong rapport is essential to team success. Communication and respect are at the heart of building common and strong bonds. Open door policies are not only necessary, but also essential. True team cohesion is then developed.

The greatest form of reinforced discipline that is critical to accomplishing goals is The Golden Rule: Treat others as you want to be treated. Honesty, integrity, and good communication skills among team members must be present and fully expected. When we set a high standard, we need to live up to it and encourage others to maintain it. I know too many people who do not set high standards, so they end up with mediocrity or, worse yet, low standards—not expecting or demanding much from themselves or others.

People want to be challenged. People want to succeed, and they want to win. But not enough of us are setting or maintaining high standards, therefore cheating ourselves and others of realizing how good we can actually be. We have to challenge ourselves every day by asking, "What do I want? What can I accomplish? What makes me really happy?" We need to do this not once in a while, but every day. This is called taking initiative and being self-motivated. We have to learn to push ourselves.

The truth will not only set you free, but you will also never struggle to remember what you said or did. Greater opportunity is always available with every step taken and every decision made to help you move forward. The power of appreciation and gratitude needs to also be practiced. I'm amazed that many people have a difficult time showing appreciation and gratitude to one another. Why is that? Are we afraid that by complimenting someone or genuinely showing gratitude that it makes us look weak? It's actually opposite of that.

Gratitude is one of the most powerful team building tools that you can have, yet it is not demonstrated nearly enough today. Gratitude doesn't cost you anything to give to someone, but the rewards and benefits can be immeasurable. A little appreciation goes a long, long way. Don't be one of those people who feels that someone owes you something. Or that people should be grateful to you just for being with them, that it's their privilege that you are around. What kind of attitude is that? It's a stinky, arrogant attitude. But it's more common than you think.

People seem to have a hard time with basic manners today. When did we stop saying "Please" and "Thank you" to one another? Basic manners and etiquette seem to not be important or practiced as much today as in the past. Why is that? Are we lazy? Did someone not teach us manners? Too many people walk around with the attitude that someone owes them something. "I've had a hard time in my life—everyone owes me. Life has not been fair to me—everyone owes me."

Recently, I came out of a restaurant, and as I came out the door, several people at that very moment were about to come in. What should I do? I held the door for them so that they could enter the restaurant before I left. Both men and women filed through the door as I held it, and I ended up standing there for a solid minute to let them in, not thinking of walking out until they all had entered. But as person after person, young after old kept coming through the door into the restaurant, it was very annoying that not *one* single person even nodded to me or verbally said, "Thank you." I guess I owed them the fact that I would hold the door.

Everyone, listen to me carefully as I am as blunt and straight forward as I can be. No one owes you anything! Life is not fair! Bad things happen to good people! The "everybody owes me" attitude is a selfish one to have. Get over yourself! Nobody owes you anything. Stop feeling entitled! Start expressing appreciation and gratitude for the many good things that you have. Get involved in life. Be a leader in appreciation and gratitude. Your modeling of this behavior to everyone around can be a powerful example to help ignite a burning desire inside each member of your team. Leaders should want it no other way. The collective improvement of the group of individuals is what *team* is all about. The great rugby player Percy Montgomery summarized it clearly, "It is never about personal goals, it's about the team."[2] Leaders, continue to prepare your team by serving and leading by example! When we come together we have limitless compassion as we lay down all our differences. That's great leadership! It's *you*, *me*, and *we*!

Chapter 7

THE MOMENT . . . !

··· ——————— ···

Everyone has experienced a moment or moments that have been life-changing (defining). When we identify the conflict, define the issue, and know the cause, we have a better chance at overcoming. In the words of my favorite waitress from the restaurant that my family goes to after church on Sunday, "We have all done negative things just to feel better about ourselves. We all look for moments of hope!" Truly she understands the whys behind the whats! This is why she is successful in overcoming her issues. My hope is that this book has been the *epiphany* you have been looking for. I know you now realize how every moment and every person matters. Every moment and every person has the potential to change not only his own life but also the lives of others.

Oftentimes our pain, challenges, and even failures move us to look inside where we find the greatest ability to help and assist others. I'm humbled that I have had the honor of impacting lives through speaking engagements and authoring books, as well as television and personal appearances. I have met so many amazing people in my travels who are from all walks of life. I like meeting people so much that hopefully, I may be that defining moment in the lives of others. We all need that affirmation, that confirmation, and that hope—the epiphany that all is going to be well.

There was a recent time in my life when I was faced with some very difficult adversities: having an issue with my neighbor and my two sisters being diagnosed with breast cancer. That was a tough time. Entering the New Year, I was extremely worried and concerned about these issues and hoping that somehow everything would turn out well in the end. One morning in January, Martin Luther King Day to be exact, I read an email that was sent to me seemingly out of the blue. The man's name who sent it to me was Moses Veigh, from California. He was a man I truly looked up to. He recently passed away, but not before he impacted millions of lives around the world through his work with Ambassadors Ministry. The first time Moses came to my house, my younger son, who was eight years old at the time, innocently said, "Dad, is that the same Moses from the Bible who wears the dress and carries that big stick?" What could I say? I still remember his innocent little eyes looking up at me. It's true. Kids do say the "darnedest things."

Moses emailed me late the night before to tell me he was thinking about me and praying for me. He wanted me to look at a particular scripture passage in the Bible—from the Book of Joshua, Chapter 1, verses 5 through 9. I truly respected Moses's thoughts and opinions, so I opened my Bible and turned to the scripture passage that he wanted me to read. I read the words all the way up to verse 9. Verse 9, of all the verses, jumped right off the page at me, as if it smacked me in the face. The New International Version translation read, "...be strong and courageous. Do not be afraid; do not be discouraged, for the LORD your God will be with you wherever you go." Wow! Did I just read what I thought I read? I read it again, "...be strong and courageous. Do not be afraid; do not be discouraged, for the LORD your God will be with you wherever you go." Moses truly sensed and divinely heard this message that was passed on to me. He knew what I needed at that particular time, especially with the adversity I was facing. I was really thrilled and encouraged by this timely message.

Later that day, my wife, Suzy, was going to take our son Aron to our favorite "French discount department store, *Tar-Jay*," A.K.A. Target in English. Aron planned to take some of his leftover Christmas present money and buy some video games. I asked Suzy to drop me off at the beach on her way to Target. My intention was that I would both walk and jog back home from the point that she dropped me off, which was a few miles from our house. Moses's revelation had gotten me so excited that I had to exercise to burn up some of my newfound energy. I felt like I'd had a shot of adrenaline. I was the Energizer Bunny times ten. The weather was perfect. It was a nice, comfortable 72 degree winter day on January 19. This is precisely why we live in the Tampa area on the west coast of Florida. I love to joke with my friends in New York and other northern parts of the country, that they also enjoy 72 degree winter weather on January 19...it's 36 degrees in the morning and 36 degrees in the evening. LOL!

I was walking on the beach on my way home, talking on the phone, and enjoying the beautiful weather. I noticed in the short distance a young man standing on the beach looking westward toward the Gulf of Mexico. I was walking north. He had long hair, wearing jean shorts but no shirt. For some reason I was drawn toward him. As I began to approach him, he saw me out of the corner of his eye. He began to slightly turn in my direction. "Wow! Look at that!" On the left side of his chest I noticed an amazing, absolutely remarkable tattoo. It was something so well done, it could have been in a picture frame hanging on the wall. It was an amazingly beautiful tattoo of a lion. The lion was leaning on its back paws, looking out with its mane blowing majestically in the wind. It was stunning to see! As I proceeded even closer toward him, he completely turned fully in my direction and immediately my jaw dropped. What? I couldn't believe what I was seeing. I started to rub my eyes, saying, "No way, no way, and no way!" I ran up to him, grabbed him by the arms and started to shake him. I said, "Do you believe in God, do you believe in fate, and do you believe in faith?" His excited, but troubled response back to me was, "I do, I do, I do. Now let go of me." I thought to myself, "You've got to be kidding me! This is unbelievable what I am seeing." Tattooed on the center of his chest were the words, "Be strong and courageous...Joshua 1:9!"

I introduced myself to him and told him about the scripture my friend Moses had sent to me, and that I had read it earlier that morning. He went on to tell me that he currently lived in Cleveland, Ohio. He was visiting some friends about one hour north of where we were standing on the beach. I asked, "What are you doing all the way down here if your friends live farther north?" He told me that they were driving him nuts, and he wanted to get away. I explained how we have "thirty miles of beaches" in this area. "Why did you choose this exact location?" He told me that when he was married he and his wife absolutely loved this area of the beach. I said to him, "But why did you choose this specific section of the beach to come to today?" He thought for a moment, and then he replied, "I don't know.

I was driving and just happened to pick this parking area. No particular reason, I guess." All I could say inside my head was, "Oh, my goodness! What a miracle. He just happened to pick this exact area. No particular reason?" He went on to tell me that he got his tattoo after his brother Joshua passed away. He explained that, "It was my brother's favorite scripture." When I experience these kinds of moments, I look up, smile, and say, "I know that was You, God! Thank You for the wink!"

Let me close by saying this—You never know *where*, you never know *when*, and you never know *how* you will experience an epiphany—like God winking at you. He loves you and thinks about you all day and all night. God is *Father God* not the Godfather! It's that unmistakable and sudden realization, and the light goes on! It all makes sense. So all I can say to you is: be *open*, be *alert*, and be *aware*! Remember, life is measured in moments! Your positive defining moment is coming! Why? It's simple. *You matta! You matta! You matta! You matter!*

Epilogue

QUOTES TO LIVE BY!

... ———————— ...

66To be a Christian means to forgive the inexcusable because God has forgiven the inexcusable in you.99[1]

—C. S. Lewis

66Forgiveness is not an occasional act, it is a constant attitude.99[2]

—Martin Luther King Jr.

66To err is human, to forgive, divine.99[3]

—Alexander Pope

66From what we get, we can make a living; what we give, however, makes a life.99[4]

—Arthur Ashe

"The truth is, unless you let go, unless you forgive yourself, unless you forgive the situation, unless you realize that the situation is over, you cannot move forward."[5]

—Steve Maraboli

"One of the keys to happiness is a bad memory."[6]

—Rita Mae Brown

"True forgiveness is when you can say, 'Thank you for that experience.'"[7]

—Oprah Winfrey

"The weak can never forgive. Forgiveness is the attribute of the strong."[8]

—Mahatma Gandhi

"Forgiveness is not about forgetting. It is about letting go of another person's throat. Forgiveness does not excuse anything."[9]

—Wm. Paul Young

"Forgiveness is the fragrance that the violet sheds on the heel that has crushed it."[10]

—Mark Twain

"We are all mistaken sometimes; sometimes we do wrong things, things that have bad consequences. But it does not mean we are evil, or that we cannot be trusted ever afterward."[11]

—Alison Croggon

"People have to forgive. We don't have to like them, we don't have to be friends with them, we don't have to send them hearts in text messages, but we have to forgive them, to overlook, to forget. Because if we don't we are tying rocks to our feet, too much for our wings to carry!"[12]

—C. JoyBell C.

"Forgiveness has nothing to do with absolving a criminal of his crime. It has everything to do with relieving oneself of the burden of being a victim—letting go of the pain and transforming oneself from victim to survivor."[13]

—C. R. Strahan

"I think that if God forgives us we must forgive ourselves. Otherwise, it is almost like setting up us as a higher tribunal than Him."[14]

—C. S. Lewis

"The willingness to forgive is a sign of spiritual and emotional maturity. Imagine a world filled with individuals willing both to apologize and to accept an apology."[15]

—Gordon B. Hinckley

"Grudges are for those who insist that they are owed something; forgiveness, however, is for those who are substantial enough to move on."[16]

—Criss Jami

"When you forgive, you love; when you love, God's light shines upon you."[17]

—Jon Krakauer

"Pass over the mistakes of others."[18]

—Mother Teresa

"As I walked out the door toward the gate that would lead to my freedom, I knew if I didn't leave my bitterness and hatred behind, I'd still be in prison."[19]

—Nelson Mandela

"Be the one who nurtures and builds. Be the one who has an understanding and a forgiving heart, one who looks for the best in people. Leave people better than you found them."[20]

—Marvin J. Ashton

"Forgiveness is an act of the will, and the will can function regardless of the temperature of the heart."[21]

—Corrie ten Boom

"To love means loving the unlovable; to forgive means pardoning the unpardonable. Faith means believing the unbelievable. Hope means hoping when everything seems hopeless."[22]

—G. K. Chesterton

"Listen. Slide the weight from your shoulders and move forward. You are afraid you might forget, but you never will. You will forgive and remember."[23]

—Barbara Kingsolver

"Forgiveness in no way requires that you trust the one you forgive."[24]

—Wm. Paul Young

"I have always found that mercy bears richer fruits than strict justice."[25]

—Abraham Lincoln

"Because you are important, everything you do is important. Every time you forgive, the universe changes; every time you reach out and touch a heart or a life, the world changes."[26]

—Wm. Paul Young

"What was the point of being able to forgive, when deep down, you both had to admit you'd never forget?"[27]

—Jodi Picoult

"Always forgive, but never forget, else you will be a prisoner of your own hatred, and doomed to repeat your mistakes forever."[28]

—Wil Zeus

"The practice of forgiveness is our most important contribution to the healing of the world."[29]

—Marianne Williamson

"I have learned that the person I have to ask for forgiveness from the most is: myself. You must love yourself. You have to forgive yourself."[30]

—C. JoyBell C.

"Love may forgive all infirmities and love still in spite of them: but Love cannot cease to will their removal."[31]

—C. S. Lewis

"Inner peace can be reached only when we practice forgiveness. Forgiveness is letting go of the past, and is therefore the means for correcting our misperceptions."[32]

—Gerald G. Jampolsky

"Be aware of who you are. Eliminate the negatives from your mind. Expect the best from yourself and others. *That equals success!*"

—Unknown

"Be nice to the people on your way up because you'll meet them on your way down!"[33]

—Wilson Mizner

"I would rather shoot for the top and just miss, then shoot for the middle and make it!"[34]

—John Osteen

"The achievements of an organization are the results of the combined efforts of each individual!"[35]

—Vince Lombardi

"Tell me and I forget. Teach me and I remember. *Involve* me and I learn."[36]

—Ben Franklin

"God is always good. He is *for* you not against you."[37]

—Unknown

"We can't always control or change our circumstances, but we can change or control our *perspective.*"

—Unknown

"Don't stay focused on the opposition or how impossible it looks. Don't consider the negative circumstances, start considering your God. Remind Him of what He said. All through the day, let His promises keep playing in your mind."

—Joel Osteen

ENDNOTES

...——...

CHAPTER 1

1. Eleanor Roosevelt, *This Is My Story*, 1937.

2. Kathryn Stockett, *The Help* (2011), ://www.goodreads.com
/work/quotes/4717423-the-help.

3. Sylvester Stallone, www.inquisir.com/1413920/sylvester
-stallone-auditioned-for-star-wars-expendables-star-admits-hed
-have-looked-bad-in-spandex (accessed May 11, 2015).

4. *Rocky Balboa* (2006), www.imdb.com/title/tt0479143/quotes
(accessed May 11, 2015).

CHAPTER 2

1. http://www.lyricstop.com/albums/natashabedingfield
/unwritten.html (accessed May 11, 2015).

CHAPTER 3

1. www.firstunitarianhamilton.org/sermons
/2010Sept19Forgiveness.pdf (accessed May 12, 2015).

2. 1988 Gallup Poll in conjunction with the Society of the Scientific Study of Religion and the Religion Research Association. www.gallup.com/poll/8944/War-Changed-Prayer-Habits-Many -Americans.aspx (accessed May 12, 2015).

3. http://www.brainyquote.com/quotes/quotes/e/epictetus149126 .html (accessed May 12, 2015).

4. *The Lion King* (1994) http://www.imdb.com/title/tt0110357 /quotes (accessed May 12, 2015).

CHAPTER 5

1. Foreigner, "I Want to Know What Love Is" (1984), www.lyricsfreak.com/f/foreigner/I+want+to+know+what+love +is_20054919.html (accessed May 13, 2015).

2. *Remember the Titans* (2000), http://www.imdb.com/title /tt0210945/quotes (accessed May 13, 2015).

3. The Monkees, "For Pete's Sake," www.azlyrics.com/lyrics /monkees/forpetessake.html (accessed May 13, 2015).

CHAPTER 6

1. Red Hot Chili Peppers, "Give It Away" (1991), www.metrolyrics.com/give-it-away-lyrics-red-hot-chili-peppers .html (accessed May 14, 2015).

2. Percy Montgomery, news.bbc.co.uk/sport2/hi/rugby_union /welsh7451593.stm (accessed May 14, 2015).

EPILOGUE

1. C. S. Lewis, www.beliefnet.com/Quotes/Christian/C/C-S
-Lewis/To-Be-A-Christian-Means-To-Forgive-The-Inexcusable.aspx
(accessed May 15, 2015).

2. Martin Luther King Jr., www.goodreads.com/quotes/57037
-forgiveness-is-not-an-occasional-act-it-is-a-constant (accessed May
15, 2015).

3. Alexander Pope, *An Essay on Criticism*, Part II (1711),
www.quotecounterquote.com/2010/12/to-err-is-human-to-forgive
-divine.html (accessed May 15, 2015).

4. Arthur Ashe, www.brainyquote.com/quotes/quotes/a
/arthurashe105661.html (accessed May 15, 2015).

5. Steve Maraboli, www.goodreads.com/author/quotes/4491185
.Steve_Maraboli (accessed May 15, 2015).

6. Rita Mae Brown, www.quotationspage.com/quote/1254.html
(accessed May 15, 2015).

7. Oprah Winfrey, www.verybestquotes.com/true-forgiveness
-quotes-by-oprah-winfrey/ (accessed May 15, 2015).

8. Mahatma Gandhi, www.brainyquote.com/quotes/quotes/m
/mahatmagan121411.html (accessed May 15, 2015).

9. Wm. Paul Young, *The Shack: Where Tragedy Confronts Eternity*
(California: Windblown Media, 2007).

10. Mark Twain, www.brainyquote.com/quotes/quotes/m
/marktwain109919.html (accessed May 15, 2015).

11. Alison Croggon, www.goodreads.com/author/quotes/32401
.Alison_Croggon (accessed May 15, 2015).

12. C. JoyBell C., www.wisdomquotesandstories.com/people -have-to-forgive/ (accessed May 15, 2015).

13. C. R. Strahan, *The Roan Maverick* (Amazon: BookSurge Publishing, 2006), 162.

14. C. S. Lewis, chroniclesofcslewis.com/433/2014/01/15/ (accessed May 15, 2015).

15. Gordon B. Hinckley, *Standing for Something: 10 Neglected Virtues That Will Heal Our Hearts and Homes* (New York: Three Rivers Press, 2001) 86.

16. Criss Jami, *Salomé: In Every Inch In Every Mile*, (Amazon: CreateSpace Independent Publishing Platform, 2011) 103.

17. Jon Krakauer, *Into the Wild* (New York: Villard Books, 1996).

18. Mother Teresa, *The Joy in Loving: A Guide to Daily Living* (New York: Penguin Putnam, Inc., 2000) 406.

19. Nelson Mandela, www.cfact.org/2013/12/06/quotes-from -nelson-mandela-1918-2013/ (accessed May 15, 2015).

20. Marvin J. Ashton, www.lovequoteslib.com/marvin-j -ashton/2741/ (accessed May 16, 2015).

21. Corrie ten Boom, *Tramp for the Lord*, Mass Market version (New York: Jove Books, 1986) 55.

22. G. K. Chesterton, www.brainyquote.com/quotes/quotes/g /gilberttkc156949.html (accessed May 16, 2015).

23. Barbara Kingsolver, www.goodreads.com/author /quotes/3541.Barbara_Kingsolver (accessed May 16, 2015).

24. Wm. Paul Young, www.goodreads.com/author /quotes/806593.Wm_Paul_Young (accessed May 16, 2015).

25. Abraham Lincoln, speech in Washington D.C., 1865. www.quotationspage.com/quote/3279.html (accessed May 16, 2015).

26. Wm. Paul Young, *The Shack: Where Tragedy Confronts Eternity* (California: Windblown Media, 2007) 235.

27. Jodi Picoult, *The Tenth Circle*, (New York: Washington Square Press, 2006) 103.

28. Wil Zeus, *Sun Beyond the Clouds* (Amazon: CreateSpace Independent Publishing Platform, 2010) 105.

29. Marianne Williamson, www.brainyquote.com/quotes /quotes/m/mariannewi138711.html (accessed May 16, 2015).

30. C. JoyBell C., www.goodreads.com/quotes/tag/forgive -yourself (accessed May 16, 2015).

31. C. S. Lewis, www.goodreads.com/work/quotes/2976220 -the-problem-of-pain (accessed May 16, 2015).

32. Gerald G. Jampolsky, *Love Is Letting Go of Fear* (California: Celestial Arts, 1979) 35.

33. Wilson Mizner, www.brainyquote.com/quotes/authors/w /wilson_mizner.html (accessed May 16, 2015).

34. John Osteen

35. Vince Lombardi, www.brainyquote.com/quotes/quotes/v /vincelomba36290.html (accessed May 16, 2015).

36. Ben Franklin, www.brainyquote.com/quotes/quotes/b /benjaminfr38997.html (accessed May 16,2015).

37. Unknown, based on Romans 8:31.

ABOUT THE AUTHOR

Bobby Petrocelli, author, educator, and one of the most sought-after motivational speakers in the country, shares his message with people from all walks of life and every generation. He combines both his expertise and his riveting personal experience to inspire and motivate people to make the right choices in life. Bobby's life is a testimony of how one can turn pain and tragedy into triumph, hope, and victory. A drunk driver crashing through his bedroom wall, severely injuring him and instantly killing his wife, is his unforgettable story of courage, determination, and forgiveness. "*Every moment* has the power to not only impact my life but the life of others! Every moment matters!"

In addition to this book, Bobby has authored and co-authored seventeen different educational and motivational books with over one million in circulation; including: *Triumph Over Tragedy, 10 Seconds Will Change Your Life Forever, 10 Seconds Is Changing Lives Forever, The Making of Unshakable Character, Unshakable Character, Lead Now—or Step Aside,* and other titles in the Teen Power Series.

He has been featured on every major TV and radio affiliate. His story has been aired in over one hundred countries as well as numerous newspapers, magazines, and other printed media.

Bobby has won the prestigious Telly Award, presented by the organization that produces the Emmy Award, for his programs on overcoming.

Bobby has been described as "a heart above the rest." His zest for life and sincere love for people is communicated clearly in his message. "If you want to experience *love*, do loving things!" Those who hear Bobby speak or read his authored material always leave energized and motivated by his story and refreshed by his charismatic personality. He never fails to captivate his audience with his expertise and powerful message. Mr. Petrocelli has been described as real, relatable, and relevant as his message screams out, "You Matter!"

He shares the secrets and principles of enduring faith, hope, and love in overcoming the adversities that life may bring.

"How we respond to these adversities is of utmost importance." "It's never too late to recalculate!" "Success is based on what you do to help others reach their destiny!"

Bobby is a Certified Speaking Professional (CSP), the highest earned designation of the National Speaking Association and International Federation of Professional Speakers. He has become one of their most sought after speakers.

Bobby holds a master's degree in counseling and a Bachelor of Science degree in health and physical education.

Bobby likes having a good time and loves people. He enjoys traveling the great outdoors—hiking, swimming, boating, and other water sports. But his greatest joy is spending time with the three most important people in his life: his beautiful wife, Suzy, and their two sons, Alec and Aron.

CONTACT
INFORMATION

PHONE

1-800-547-7933

EMAIL

Bobby@10seconds.org

WEBSITES

Bobbypetrocelli.com
10seconds.org
Youmatter10.com
Teamyoumatter.com
Theyoumattermovement.com
Youmatternation.com

INSTAGRAM

@bobbypetrocelli

TWITTER

@bobbypetrocelli

FACEBOOK

Bobby Petrocelli